Hello...
Great to have you on board!

Hi I'm John Banks, and I would llike to say a massive thank you for buying this guide to Side Hustles book!

My mission is to help you start earning a side income. You can start pretty much as soon as you have finished reading this book! It will certainly give you some ideas!

I run my own website agency, owner of several other sites and blogs, writer and business owner. I have also been a consultant for multi million dollar companies but now my attention has turned to helping others create additional income streams.

This guide will contain several side hustles varying in difficulty and reward but all are achievable with the right mindset.

Head over to Instagram and follow me on there and message me when you want to. We are in this together!

 @sideincomeman

Disclaimer & Boring Stuff

Before I get to the main section of the book I have to disclose that just like on the website I sometimes use affiliate links in the material.

This means that a link may lead you to a site or product that is not my own. If you ever did decide to buy from them then I may get a commission as it's a recommendation from me.

This is common business practice and happens all over the world in many sectors. The online space is no different.

Also, there are no guarantees that you will get the same results as I have done over the years with some of these side hustles, you may get worse, you may get better.

I cannot predict the level of effort and hustle you are going to put into this. But these methods in this book are tried and tested and proven to be successful.

As with anything in business or personal life - **DO YOUR OWN RESEARCH.**

With all that jargon out the way, lets dive in!

Introduction

"The Dream Is Free, But The Hustle Is Real"

 @sideincomeman

Introduction

People are starting to feel the crunch more and more these days. It may not be the fault of them, or it may be. We live in a consumer world now – a world where people compare via their Facebook feeds.

It's not a truly accurate portrayal of the world we "should" be living in.

The world we should be living in should be one where we care for those that matter first and foremost. Look after your families and friends.

What am I getting at here?

Well, if we all decided to live off the grid in the woods and be happy with our mud huts and having to fish and hunt for food each day, living off our land and making do with whatever fun activities you can make up then the world would be a happier place.

It's not though.

People like stuff. People like holidays. People like a new phone every 6 months. People like 300 TV channels.

All of that comes at a price.

Of course, I am being a little jokey here. Everyone likes a bit more. It's what we have become as humans. There is nothing wrong with a bit of the good life.

What is the point of this book?

This book is aimed at anyone who wants a little bit more in terms of financial comfort. Throughout this book you will find ten proven methods on how you can earn a healthy side income stream.

Use it however you wish. But if by taking action and getting results it can help you to pay a bill each month, buy a new car, repay a loan or even land you a new full-time income stream then it would have fulfilled its reason for me writing it.

The methods in this book range in difficulty. Some are VERY easy while some will require some more effort on your part.

The side hustles are rated 1 to 5 stars in difficulty. 1 star being the easiest to start!

Unfortunately, most people will probably read this and do nothing, take no action at all and go on moaning about how the TV subscription has gone up or the gas and electric is £20 more per month this year.

These things happen. This is the real world. (In its current bad state)

Please do try some of these, pick one that suits you and go for it. After all –that's why you got this book in the first place isn't it?

After reading this there really will be no excuses.

Sadly, though many people will still find them. I hope you are not one of them.

So on to the methods. I want this book to become a reference for you, some of the methods may contain links to further reading, tools, support etc.

Each method will have a star rating next to them. The lower the star the easier the method.

Here we go.

"DON'T BE AFRAID TO FAIL, BE AFRAID NOT TO TRY"

#1 eBay

User Level

"For me the king of the entry level side hustles, one you can turn on and off as you please"

Everyone will have something they can sell on eBay. It is one of the simplest ways to start your side income empire. You can start by selling unwanted clothes, toys, games, music or go even further afield and venture into the collectables and antiques markets.

I will cover more specific details within eBay as we go on but eBay in general is a great way to make some quick money.

Sign up for an account and get to work listing any small product. It's not important straight away how much money you make.

What is important here is that you learn the steps involved in getting an item listed.

Trust me, if you have never "done" eBay before make sure you download the app to your phone as the notifications of your item receiving bids will be very addictive.

In fact, you'll probably turn it off after a while!

You can literally get started with just your phone and a PayPal account.

For more eBay success stories head over to sideincomeman.com/blog

Tips:

- Take as many pictures as you can. Use all the slots available to you.

- Take REALLY good pictures, nothing says bad seller more than some crappy out of focus pictures. Take your time, get some good shots of your product from different angles.

- Be descriptive. List your items with as many details as you can. If it's got any small defects be sure to say so.

Gain some feedback early! If you are new and never listed on eBay before you may want some feedback first.

You can do this by getting several things listed and making some sales or you can buy some bits from here and get good feedback this way.

Buy a few day to day items that you need anyway and you will quickly get feedback from the other sellers.

Ebay is a really scalable business. I have personally known people who have made a full time living from this platform. It's up to you.

With a little bit of budgeting and planning you can very easily get yourself up to £100's per month using this platform.

Start off selling all your stuff around your home that you no longer want. You can find out if an item is going to sell by using the 'Sold Listings' feature.

Here is how to do this using the desktop version.

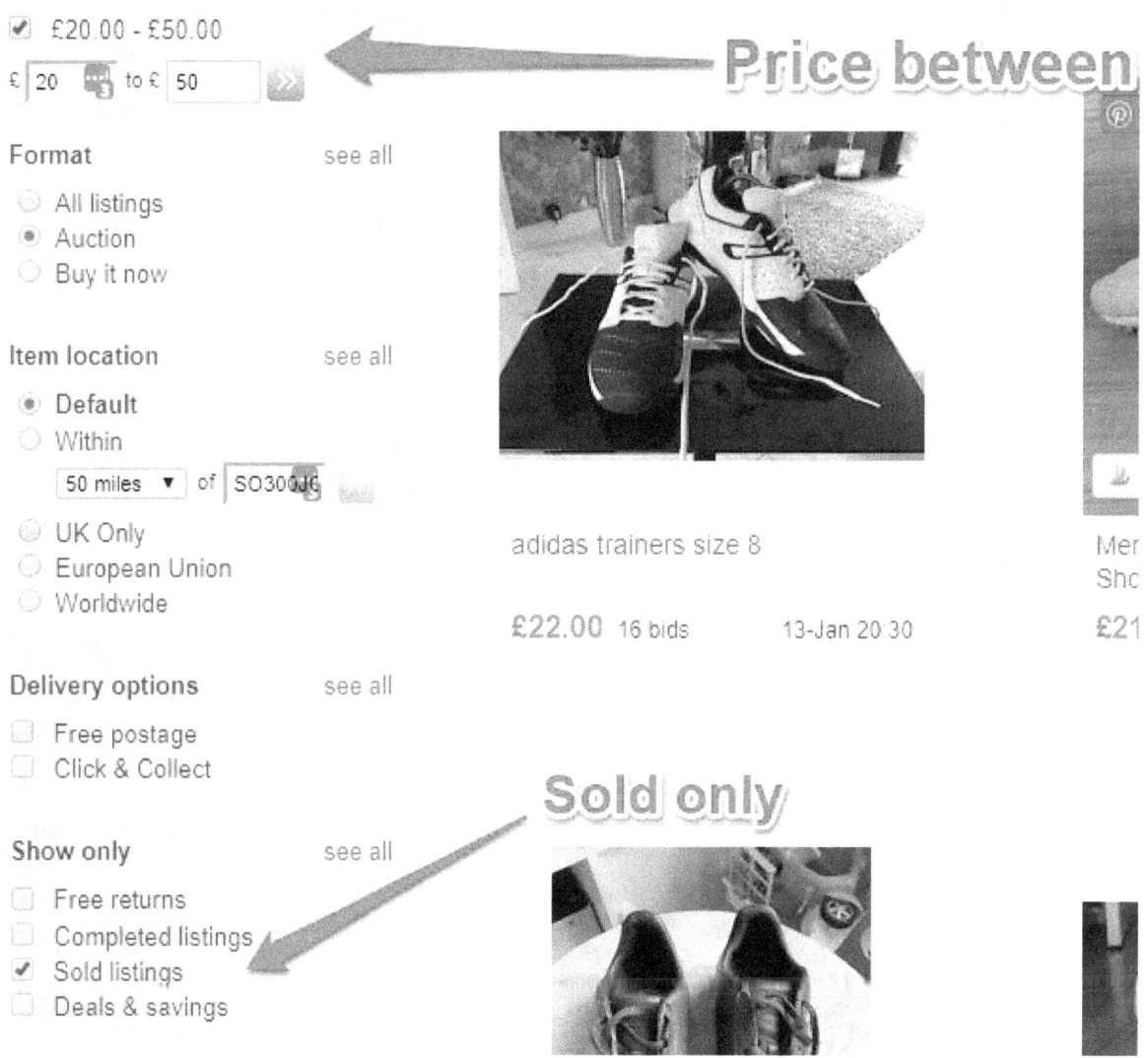

You can see from the example I have searched for "mens trainers" and I have chosen the price point between £20 and £50 and then selected "sold listings".

This will give me a great idea as to what sells in this range.

Where do I get stock from after I've sold all my stuff?

Once you have sold all your items you no longer wanted you can start to source your own stock from other outlets! This for some is just as much fun, if not more than the listing and selling.

Head off to your local charity shops or thrift stores. You will be amazed at what you can find in these shops.

Do not ignore anything. Quite often you will come across something that you think will have no value only to be surprised!

Try it. Go out with maybe £10 and see what you can find to sell for profit.

You will be surprised.

It gets easier too, after you have been selling on eBay for a while you will start to spot brands, games, old toys and other bits that you know will turn a profit.

Another great sourcing spot is car boot sales, for US readers these are a lot like garage sales. People literally give stuff away here, often these are used as a house clearance, so you can VERY often grab a bargain.

Don't give up, eBay can be daunting and often sellers can hit a brick wall, sales will go up and down. It obviously depends on how much work you are willing to put in.

But as an entry level to the side hustle there really is no better place.

With millions of users worldwide you literally have buyers waiting on tap.

£7,001.49

60-day total

266	240	471
ACTIVE	SOLD	UNSOLD

For more eBay success stories head over to sideincomeman.com/blog

#2 Amazon FBA

User Level

"Send your stock in to the Amazon warehouses and they will sell it for you!"

Again, this is another selling platform for you to sell stuff. The difference being that FBA stands for "Fulfilled By Amazon".

What does this mean?

Well, this means that Amazon will take care of the stock for you. They will take care of the shipping, handling, packaging when you have an order.

They will even take care of any customer returns issues you may have.

Sound good?

It is, but they are obviously not going to do all that for free. They take a fee for everything that is sold, they also take a storage fee and on top of this there is a monthly fee just for selling on their platform.

The monthly fee is £30 a month. Or, you can opt for a smaller account and they will take £1 on top for every item you sell.

These are the two options you have.

I realise that having fees like this won't be for everyone, but you have to weigh up the costs versus your time.

With Amazon FBA your **main focus** is sourcing stock.

Once you have some items you literally send them all in a box to the Amazon fulfilment centre and they will take care of the rest for you.

All your stock will be processed and sit on a shelf until somebody buys it.

Your cut of the sale is worked out, their fees are taken out and you are automatically paid every two weeks.

I know many people who make a very nice side income (some people full time income) from using this platform.

Like any platform you are planning to sell on start with items in and around your home.

You will need to download the Amazon Seller app. Once you have done this you can go around scanning items to see if they are worthy to send in and what asking price you could get.

For a complete step by step guide to getting started with Amazon FBA go here: sideincomeman.com/fba

What are good items to start with?

One area which requires no approval is books. I say approval because some categories require approval first. This can vary from a simple email request to much more.

Amazon as a company started as a book store. So, this is where you should start too.

Books are still huge business and second-hand sellers make up a large proportion of all the books sold on Amazon every day.

Check the non-fiction books you have around your home. Textbooks, guidebooks, tutorials, anything like that would be a good starting block.

Once you have enough items for a box then you can prepare your shipment and send it in.

After you have sourced a few books move on to any item that is still in its original box. Things like console games, DVDS, board games etc.

You'll be surprised. You may even find a few items that you would not think would even sell but they will.

For a complete step by step guide to getting started with Amazon FBA go here: sideincomeman.com/fba

How do I know it will sell?

Every item that you can sell on Amazon has a rank within its category. This rank is defined by how many sales it's had.

So, you can get an idea for something based on this number. For example, a book ranked 743 against a book ranked 12,323,452 would sell a hell of a lot faster than the book ranked in the millions.

There are several "rules of thumb" in this marketplace for sellers but as a ball park figure you should aim for the top 1% of your category.

Take books again as an example. At the time of writing this there are around 60 million book titles listed on Amazon.

So, you should be aiming for any book that falls under the 600,000 rank mark.

This is just rule of thumb, but if you started your Amazon journey using this as a guide you will be on the right track.

Remember, each category has its own rank. So, 600,000 may be ok for a book but for a video game or beauty product it could be garbage.

The longer an item sits on the shelf the more you'll pay in storage fees to Amazon.

Don't let that last line put you off, it's a fantastic market and a great way to earn a decent side hustle.

For a complete "How To Send Your First Box In" step by step guide check out this below.

sideincomeman.com/fba

There are a few articles over on the blog of various success stories too regarding Amazon FBA.

It really can be a very healthy side income!

Days like the screenshot below are not uncommon once you build up your stock.

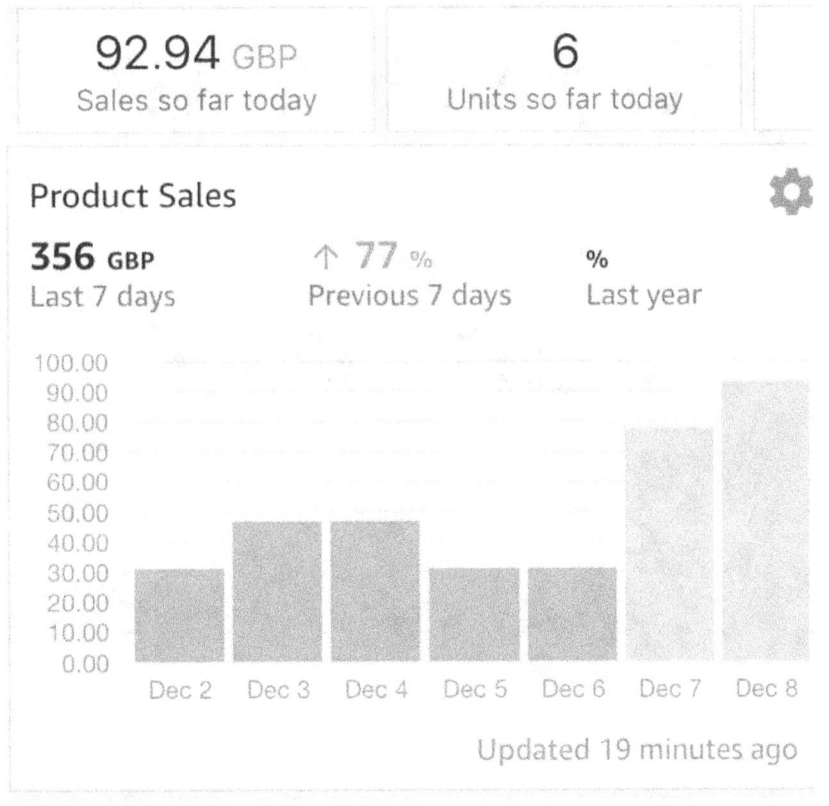

More FBA success stories over on the blog
sideincomeman.com/blog

#3 Second Hand Shoe Seller

User Level

★

"You will not believe the prices you can get for some second hand shoes"

Did you know you could make a very healthy side hustle from second-hand shoes? You could. Let's get a bit more specific now.

I have outlined a few places where you can sell stuff online. All very good marketplaces and all have their pros and cons.

Second-hand shoes are a very good thing to sell on eBay. My personal view is you need to use eBay to get the most leverage from your shoes.

If you are new to selling, then start off with one or two pairs. Maybe even run them as a low buy it now price or let them run at auction. This will pretty much guarantee you a sale.

It's not about profit here yet. The goal for you when starting out is to get familiar with the process of listing and preparing your stock.

What do I need to prepare?

I would highly recommend cleaning the shoes before listing them, you don't have to take all day doing it but spend a few minutes getting them looking their best. This is the difference between you and other sellers who don't care as much.

Make sure you take good bright photos. Nothing will get you less visits more to your listing than bad photos.

Take a look at the example here:

Then take a look at this one:

Which one do you think has the more potential to sell?

I can tell you, one of these pairs sold for £5.95 and the other pair sold for £36

(I know they are different shoes and brands but the pictures 100% do make a difference)

You are going to be competing with others in your field, so you must stand out.

What type of shoes can I sell?

You can sell shoes, trainers or boots. Whichever you like.

Just make sure you have them in the best most presentable way you can before you list them.

Men's Rare Adidas Rom White / Blue Leather Trainers Size UK 8 Classic Retro VGC

£71.00
+ Free postage

The top brands obviously stand out more than the unknown brands. Avoid any unbranded shoes, or low quality.

Here is my personal favourite men's list of brands to sell:

- Nike
- Adidas
- Asics
- New Balance
- Converse
- Edward Green
- Loake
- Churchs
- Oliver Sweeney
- Timberland
- Dr Martins

All of these if picked up for cheap (charity shops, car boot sales, discounts, clearance stock etc) can turn into a pretty profit.

If you are selling on eBay always check the completed listings first before jumping in and buying items.

Although, after a while you will have your eye in for shoes that you know will sell.

Further reading and training on this:
sideincomeman.com/shoes

How do I know how to identify a shoe?

Obviously, most shoes will come with a brand name that can be seen somewhere on the shoe. I think its best as I have said to avoid unbranded shoes.

Make sure the brand is clear, if the name or familiar markings of a shoe do not look right then it may be best to avoid selling it. You do not want to EVER sell fakes.

Another tip is to look under the tongue, especially in trainers. These will often have a "model number" somewhere on it which will help you identify it.

List as many markings and numbers as you can when you are selling them. Some people will search by these numbers so it's best to include them.

#4 Write A Blog

User Level

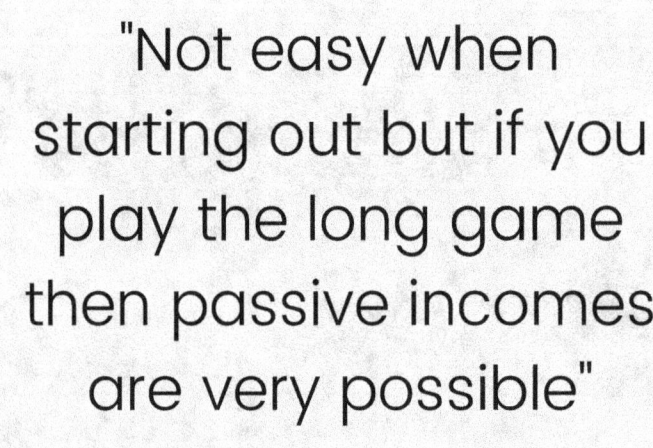

"Not easy when starting out but if you play the long game then passive incomes are very possible"

Not everyone will be familiar with the term blogging, but it is a very popular thing nowadays with many people writing blogs now as a hobby and also as a business. It's quite possible to earn a very healthy full-time income from having your own blog let alone a side income.

The trick is to get people to visit it. We call this traffic. Without traffic you could have the best blog in the world and if nobody sees it or reads it then it's pointless really.

I wanted just to outline this side hustle because many people may be put off by it thinking that writing your own blog is too complex.

It's not really. But to begin with you will need a little investment. As a minimum you will need:

- A Domain Name (The name of your website)
- A Hosting plan (Somewhere to host your website)
- A platform to build it on

A domain name can be picked up for as little as £10 for the year, often cheaper, often a little more but that is the ballpark figure for a non-premium name these days.

Next up you will need hosting. This is the company that looks after your site and makes sure that it is always online.

I use SiteGround for this, so I recommend them 100% and I wouldn't recommend any other. Trust me, I've used some bad ones before now.

You can sign up for a little as £2.75 (about $4) a month with this exclusive offer for my readers.

You can also buy the domain with them too, so it is all kept in one place.

They offer great service and can help you in getting set up if you get stuck.

Sign up with them here: sideincomeman.com/sg

If you want to learn how to build a website and add a blog to it I have you covered in my free video series here: sideincomeman.com/build-a-website/

Lets now talk about the rewarding world of blogging.

So, how do make money blogging?

There are many ways. I will outline what I consider the three main ones are here and go into more detail throughout the book on others.

Advertising

Once you have a few posts up and a few readers on your blog you can strategically place advertising on your blog. Every time anyone clicks on your ads you will receive revenue for each click. It will most likely only be pennies but even pennies per click can add up into a very nice side income if you have thousands of visitors.

Sell Stuff Online

Maybe you are an artist, maybe you make crafts, maybe you have your own fashion ideas. Having your own website allows you to sell your own products and keep all of the profits yourself. Your own website with your own pricing is a very rewarding income stream if done right.

You can also sell digital products such as eBooks, Courses plus many other downloadable content such as templates, cheatsheets, meal planners etc

Pro tip: the best thing about digital products is you only have to make them once but can sell it over and over again.....

Affiliate Sales

You don't need your own products to make money through selling items. You can become an affiliate and companies will pay you a commission to sell their products for them.

This is often the preferred method when starting out online for many as it requires no stock and handling of their own.

The blog owner will advertise the item, write a solid review maybe and then for any sale that is generated from the site they will get a commission from the sale.

Some companies pay up to 75% commissions for digital products and courses – yes, you read that right. **That means for every $100 sale of an item you would receive $75 of it.**

However, from my experience of selling digital affiliate products it is much better if you are actually a user of the product first before selling it.

Those are the three main ways to make money from a blog of your own. Advertising, selling your own stuff, selling other people's stuff.

More blogging tips and tricks on my YouTube channel: sideincomeman.com/youtube

I should point out here that blogging takes time and dedication, this is not a quick hustle. You need to be prepared to graft, put the hours in and build it up.

Your blog will need to evolve, you will need to write a lot of posts, you will need to gain followers and readers. All these things take time.

That being said, the rewards can be great. So, if you do want to get started then be prepared for the long game with this one.

Many bloggers have fulfilled a dream with theirs, changing their lives for the better.

I interviewed a full time blogger by the name of Anastasia – she shared her story on the blog of her making $3000 per month from her blog.

Check it out on the blog: sideincomeman.com/blog

#5 The Rent A Room Hustle

User Level

"Gone are the days of local newspaper ads to make money from a spare room"

Gone are the days where you had to run an ad in the local newspaper in order to get a potential new tenant for your spare room. Also, you probably had to offer up a minimum of a 6 months stay. What if the person only wanted to stay a few days, maybe just a weekend?

Well, with this method you can offer just that.

There is a relatively new method hitting the online world now with people making money from their homes. Do you have a spare room going? Maybe you had kids that have now moved out to college, maybe you have kids that have now left home altogether.

Either way if you have a spare room going you can make a very nice side hustle from it.

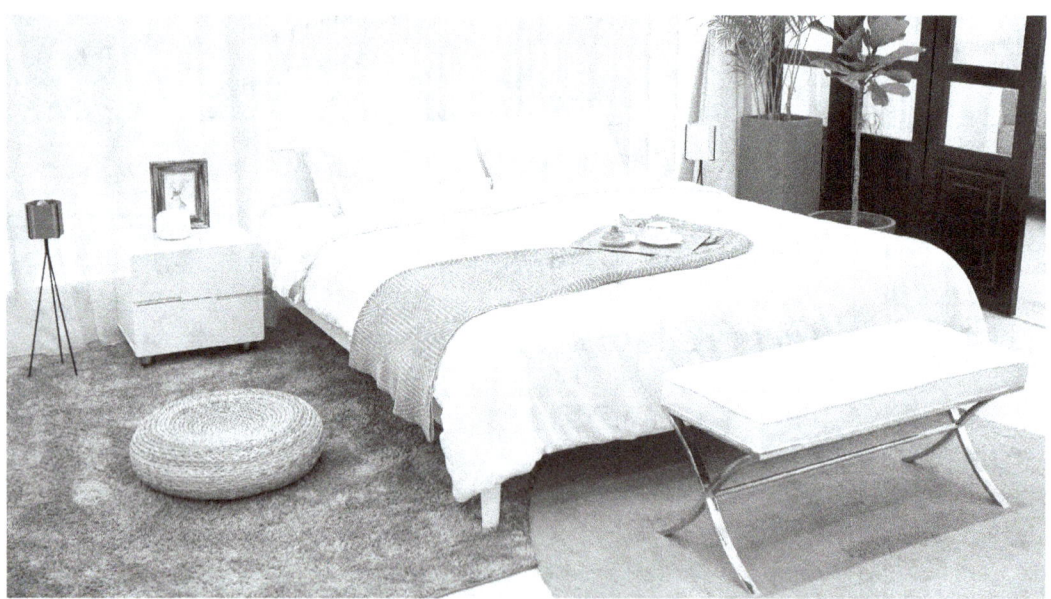

You can use a site called AirBnB. This is a website that allows people to rent out their spare rooms on a nightly basis. Think of it as a part time bed and breakfast (the breakfast part being optional).

People nowadays love to travel on a budget and their biggest expense is often the accommodation they are staying in. This is where you can step in.

Hotels in big cities for example are very expensive and they charge a premium just for the location.

If you happened to live just a few miles outside of the city you could offer up your room for rent and make a very nice side hustle from it. Especially in holiday seasons.

The great thing about this gig is it requires no start-up costs. You just must be comfortable with somebody staying in your house for a few nights.

I am sure you won't mind after the payments come in.

The beauty of using AirBnb as your broker is the contracts are binding and the payments are made through AirBnb's trusted services.

As you grow your little rented room empire you will start to get some reviews, so make your guest welcome obviously. The more reviews of high quality will increase your chances of getting repeat guests!

They also offer a smart messaging service, so you can remain in contact with your guests right up until their arrival.

You can easily make around £30 for 1 room per night.

If you opened up your rooms for just 1 week each month you would be making a nice £210 per month for something that is normally just unused space.

#6 Print On Demand T-Shirts

User Level

"There has never been a better time to get into Print on Demand!"

Print on demand is nothing new these days but in case you have not heard of it I will give you a brief overview of how it works.

Basically, it's a service that once your product sells the distributor will have it printed and dispatch it for you. So, you hold no stock, no inventory and do not have to take care of any shipping or product queries or returns (hopefully you don't get any).

Sound good? Right let's begin.

Many print on demand services started out as a sort of crowd funding exercise. In order to make the sale you had to sell x amount of a product before your product would get printed.

Teespring is probably the most famous print on demand service that followed this format. Whilst this is great and many marketers have made a very nice side hustle from this site I will be concentrating on services that will pay out even if just one product sells.

So, for every t-shirt that sells you will make a commission. Remember, you hold no stock and do none of the shipping. Your job is to come up with designs that sell and maybe market them, which is optional.

More on this later.

A rough ballpark figure is for every t-shirt you sell for $20 you can expect to make around $5 profit for you. This is not bad at all. Just 20 x sales a month will get you a $100 every month. And if the shirt is an evergreen design this will become virtually passive income. Meaning you will see these commissions time and time again with no extra work on your behalf.

What Print On Demand Services Can I Use?

There are several out there, some much better than others. I have mentioned Teespring but I am going to advise two others which I recommend you sign up for. Both are free to sign up so you have nothing to lose.

Sunfrog Shirts

I really like Sunfrog shirts, so much so that I have multiple accounts with them. It is a very user-friendly platform. Payments can be paid directly into your PayPal account every month or you can request payments quicker if you wish.

The dashboard is very easy to use. You simply select the t-shirt style you wish you use, upload your design, resize to the size you want it and then select your colours.

After your design has been submitted you can write out your description and set your pricing etc.

Other benefits of Sunfrog is they have a great selection of marketing tools where you can see your designs being worn by models and in different poses etc. It's a great tool. Some of the higher resolution images here have to be purchased for a one-off fee but they are completely optional and you do not need to buy them.

You can build a marketing campaign just by using the image of the shirt with your design on it.
Or, you can choose to do no marketing whatsoever and hope to get some organic sales from their marketplace.

Total Payout History:
$3,300.31

Merch By Amazon

Merch by Amazon is another fantastic print on demand service. By far the biggest online. The beauty of this one is you are tapping into the millions of Amazon customers. Amazon themselves do a great way of marketing your products anyway so if you are wanting to get into print on demand then you have to have one of these accounts.

Unfortunately, they do not accept new accounts straight away. Your account will need approval first and this can take several months. My advice is to sign up now and forget about it.

It only takes a few minutes to apply then they will contact you once you are accepted.

Sign up here if you want to have a go: https://merch.amazon.com/landing

Unlike Sunfrog though it's a little bit fiddlier to actually get a design up. Once you have done it a few times though you will be fine.

The images must be a specific size and depending on whether you are doing t-shirts or hoodies the size of the image changes.

I have put together a guide below showing exactly how to get your shirts listed, including any resizing that needs doing.

How To List Shirts On Amazon Merch

T-shirts sizes must be 4500 x 5400px
Hoodies sizes must be 4500 x 4050px

Take your design/image that you have created and go to **resizeimage.net**

---

1. Upload an image

Select an image from your device(Max: 100 MB & 100 MP, GIF format: 3(

Upload an image

You can upload an image in JPEG, PNG, GIF or BMP format. You may al:

2. Crop your image(optional)

Click and drag on the preview image to select your desired area, or fill in t

Enter new size dimensions. Untick "keep aspect ratio box"

Then click on RESIZE button.

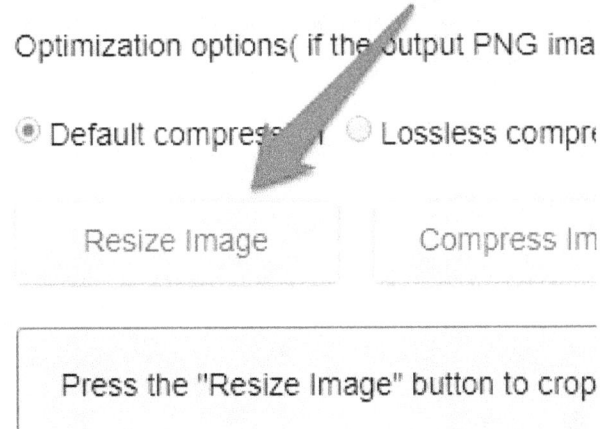

Then DOWNLOAD NEW IMAGE

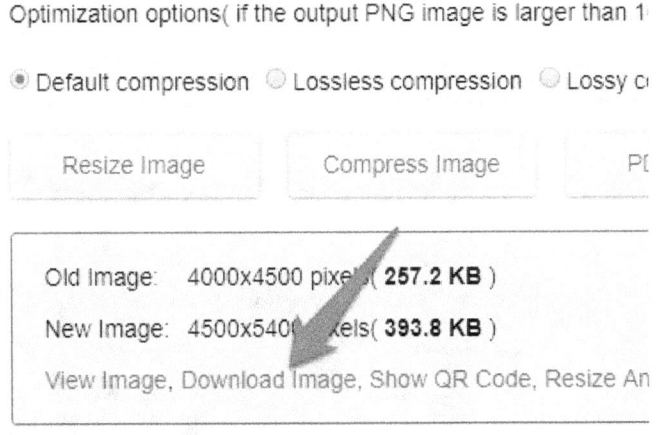

Save this to your computer somewhere.

This is the image you will need to upload to Merch.

Inside Amazon Merch

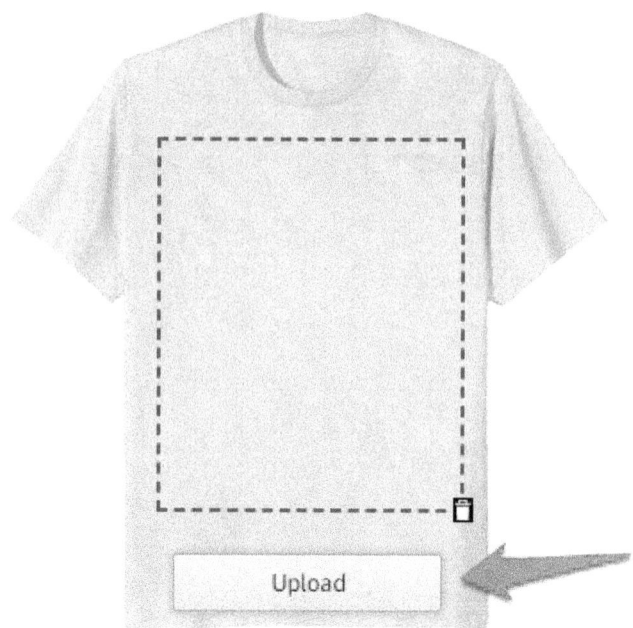

Upload and select the new resized image. Once uploaded click SAVE.

Next choose colours and price.

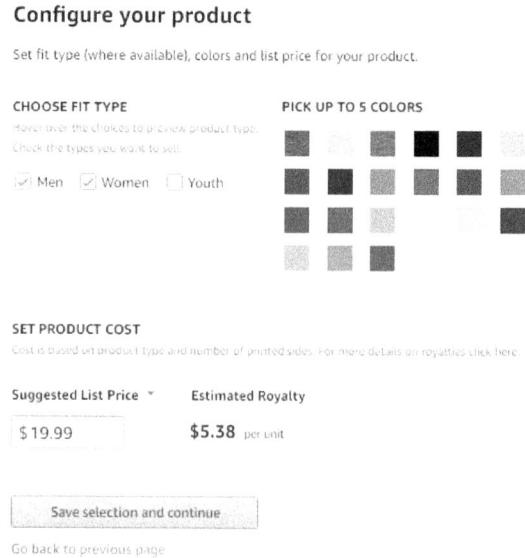

You can pick up to 5 colours, sometimes I experiment with just one or two. Sometimes I find more choice confuses people. Up to you, test it out. Same goes with price, try different price points. I would not go above $19.99 though. I have some listed for $14.99 up to $19.99

Once happy click SAVE.

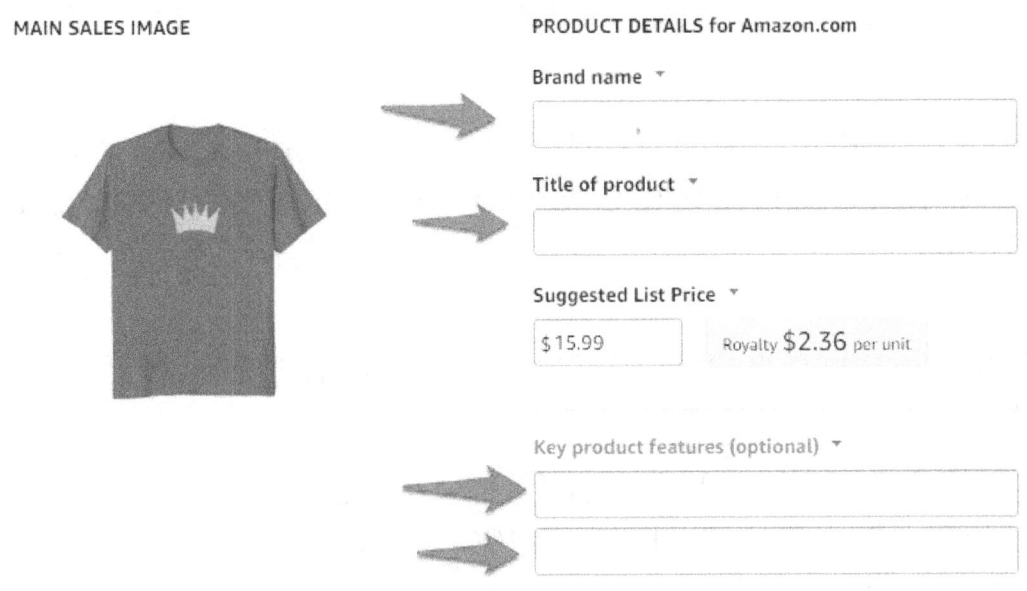

Enter brand name, title of product and key product features. These are all things which will affect search.

(The following listing is an example, there are no certainties it will sell using the example above, its just to give you an idea)

Example:

Brand Name: **BBQ T-Shirts For Men**

Title of Product: **Mens BBQ T-Shirt Summer Tees For Men**

Key product features: **Are you the BBQ king? Do you like to own the BBQ in the garden? Maybe you are one of those Dads who loves to BBQ? Then this funny BBQ T-Shirt is for you.**

Line 2: **Great gift for Dads, Sons, Uncles, People Who Love To BBQ, Friends, Colleagues. Funny birthday gift t-shirt.**

Once happy click SAVE SELECTION AND CONTINUE

Double check everything is good to go. Select SELL – Public on Amazon (If not already selected) and click on SUBMIT PRODUCT

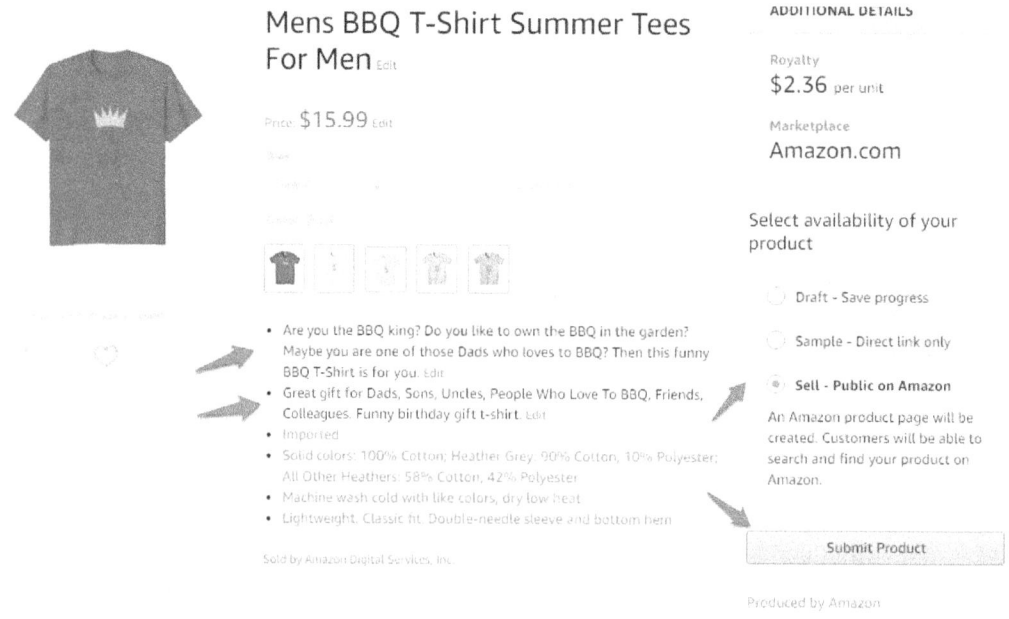

This is it.

You can do multiple listings for one design.

For example, on this you could do a BBQ King for Womens T-shirts, Mens T-shirts and Hoodies.

Making this one design into three listings.

Once the product is submitted it will take a few hours usually for it to get approval then it is live!

Merch is all about testing new designs, some work, some don't. Even the best design in the world in your eyes may sell none. Just the way it is. This doesn't stop you however relisting it and trying different keywords etc...

The main benefit is the traffic. You are tapping into a juggernaut that is Amazon, it simply has the most buyers than any online platform in the world. So, well worth applying.

They have very strict copyright rules and if any shirt design or description breaks these rules then your shirt will be removed. I do not know how many of these rule breaks you are allowed before your account becomes permanently suspended so be careful when uploading. With all print on demand services do not copy others or blatantly steal designs from big box office films or anything. That is just a disaster waiting to happen....

So what designs can I put on my shirts?

You must use your own designs or royalty free with the correct creative commons license. This is stuff that is free to use for commercial purposes. Always check here. Don't think for one minute you can just slap an image of your favourite footballer on a shirt and be done with it. It could land you in some hot mess if you kept breaking these violations.

There are many websites that offer up royalty free images free for commercial use. The one I like is one called Pixabay. (ALWAYS, ALWAYS check though the license for each image you use).

Of course, you don't have to make designs with images on, many people have made serious money with designs only with text on them.

Simple text, but has sold thousands of t-shirts.

It is about finding your audience. If a design resonates with a captive audience, then they will buy it.

Here are a few niches that have buyers in them:

- Pets
- Sports
- Hobbies
- Politics
- Food
- Workout Gear
- Seasonal
- Family
- Religion

These are just a few, in fact within each of these niches you could easily make 20 more sub-niches and this is where you should focus.

We have talked about this before. A shirt that says "I Love My Dog" is far less likely to sell than one that says "This Mom Loves Her German Shepherd". What about if you went even further. Something like "I Love God, My Family & My German Shepherd"

This is just an example but by niching down you increase your chances of making sales organically.

Designs do not have to be really complicated, its the message and how it connects to the buyers that is important.

Recent Activity	Marketplace	Products sold	Returned	Revenue	Estimated royalties
Last 7 days	.com	9	0	$179.91	$47.07
View Analyze page	.co.uk	0	0	£0.00	£0.00
	.de	0	0	€0.00	€0.00

Evergreen Shirts

These are like the Holy Grail of t-shirt designs. Evergreen shirts are designs that sell all year round. Most of the time you are not going to hit a home run with these and sell loads really quickly, but these are shirts that consistently sell a few designs each day/week/month. Once you have a nice selection of evergreen shirts you will really start to see the fruits of your labour.

Summary

Be on the lookout for design ideas all the time. You will start to see ideas everywhere. Check the magazine aisle in the supermarket, if there is a magazine out about a topic then you know 100% that there is a buyer's audience there too.

Read and watch the news, this may be where you can jump on trends and hot topics. I remember when the U.S presidential campaign was running people were making insane money from t-shirts based around the two main parties.

Basically, there are countless opportunities with t-shirt designs and with these print on demand services if you put a bit of work in, learn the ropes and don't give up you can make a very nice side income stream that can be as hands off or hands on as you want it to be.

#7 Advertising Networks On Your Blog

User Level

"Very hard, but get it right and you are pretty well set for a long time"

This side hustle does require you to have a website or blog. If you have not already got one set up and this is something that interests you then head over to my free course and get setup today.

sideincomeman.com/build-a-website

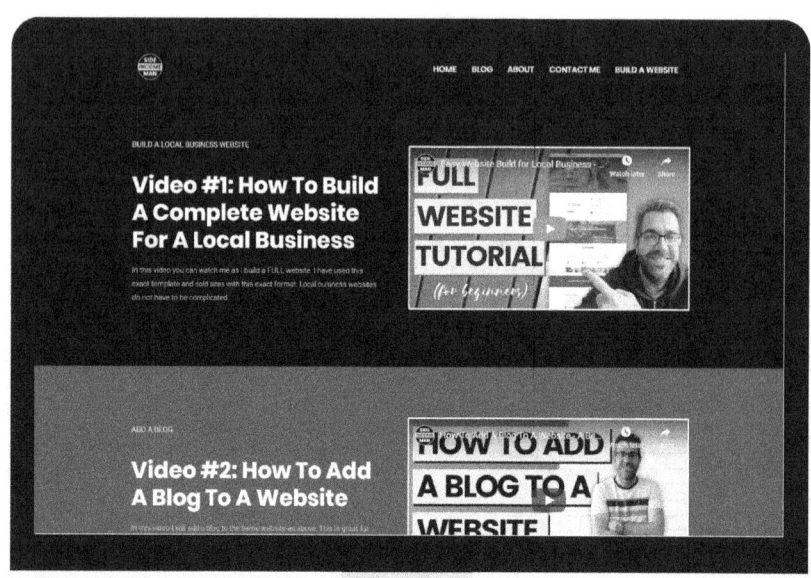

Adsense is the ad network of Google. You know when you enter a search term into Google you get listings at the top with a little "Ad" symbol next to them. This means people are paying Google essentially to have their ad there. Depending on the search term you have entered some ads can cost up to $20 per click. **Yes, you read that right, $20 per click.**

So, that client is paying Google $20 every time somebody clicks on an ad. But the hope of the client is that it converts into a buying customer so therefore paying $20 to make say $3000 on some premium home insurance is well worth it.

Why is this important for me to know?

It is important that you understand how these ad networks work and that there are vast amounts of money changing hands each day! Your job as a website owner is to get in the middle and take a small slice yourself.

You see, not only are these ads on the Google search results but also these ads show up on websites too. Have you ever been to a website looking to buy something one day and then the next time you go on another website there is an Ad showing you a similar item if not the same one again?

This is retargeting. The site you first visited knows you went there so they tailor ads for you.

As a publisher (website owner) you can earn a slice of each time someone clicks on the ad on your site.

For example:

Tim owns a fishing shop. He wants more visitors, so he pays Google $2.00 every time somebody clicks on an ad he sets up.

From this Google will take $1.60 and pay the publisher (you the website owner) $0.40.

For every click.

Now $0.40 per click may not sound a lot but again what if you could get 10 clicks per day, 100 clicks per day, maybe even a 1000 clicks per day.

It's all possible. I've seen it, I've actually done it.

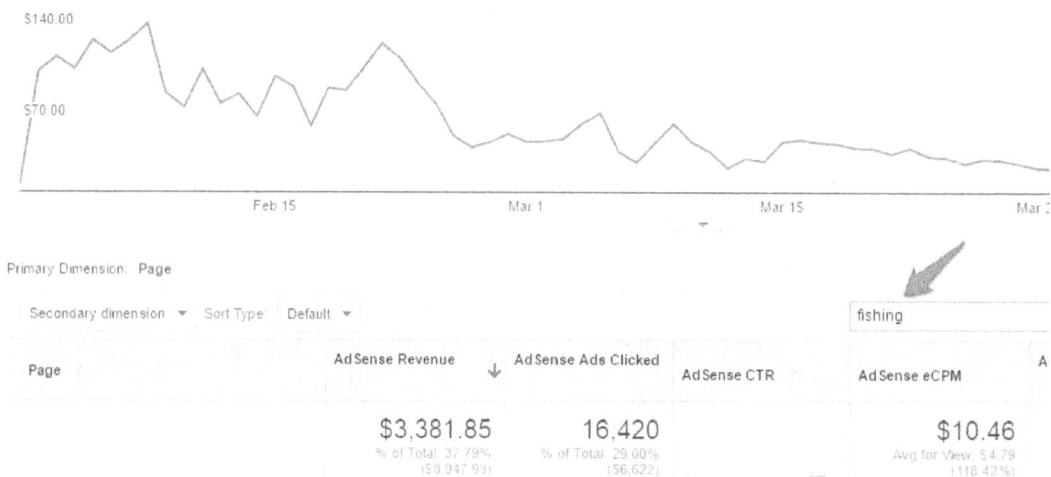

Take a modest 10 clicks at $0.40, that's $4.00 per day. That will give you around the $100 a month mark give or take a few dips.

And all this from placing some strategic ads on your website.

Once you start getting a steady flow of traffic then those posts can become almost hands off while you create new content.

Sounds easy, why isn't everyone making loads of these websites?

That is because it is not easy. This has a 5-star difficulty rating for a reason. The reason being you need a very well-established website and a whole truck load of traffic (visitors).

Getting traffic to a website is a topic for another whole book in itself. But essentially there are three main types of traffic.

1: Free traffic

This is traffic that you get for free either from the search results or from your social shares etc.

2: Paid traffic

This is traffic you pay various ad networks to show your site. It's not just Google that has ad networks, many other big players here such as Facebook have their own ad networks and they will happily take people's money to show ads for them!

3: Traffic you own.

This is by far the best type of traffic. This can be traffic from an email subscribers list or custom notifications etc. A mass newsletter sending can generate some nice quick income from your Adsense ads.

Most people will opt for the free traffic route probably due to budgeting reasons; this is fine but will naturally take you longer to earn any substantial earnings. The paid route scares people but what if you could buy traffic for $10 and make $12 back? Surely you will do this all the time right? Yes, if your budget allowed it then you should do.

Adsense is a numbers game but if you get it right it can be a very nice side hustle indeed. In fact, some websites run their entire business model around these ads and the revenue from them.

Native Advertising Networks

Much of what I will go over with this side income stream is the same as what was outlined in the Adsense method. You will need a website, and you will need some traffic.

If you already have that then great! Let's begin with this method.

This is very similar in the sense that you are going to be making money from people clicking on the ads on your website.

What are native ads and why are they different to Adsense?

Native ads are setup in the same way, in that there is a client who is paying the ad network to serve that ad somewhere. From that fee that they pay them you the publisher gets a cut every time someone clicks on one.

This is exactly the same.

But with native ads they are not going to be an ad about the last item you left in your Amazon basket, instead these usually serve as a "people are also reading" type ad.

What's Popular Now — Sponsored Links by content.ad

She Had No Idea Why the Crowd Was Cheering

Find Every Secret They Want Kept Hidden

You Won't Believe How Thin These Celebrities Used to Be

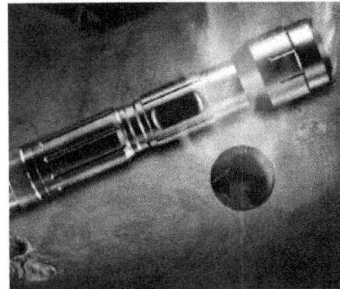
Forget Pepper Spray, All Women Need This

How This Regular Guy Learned 11 Languages

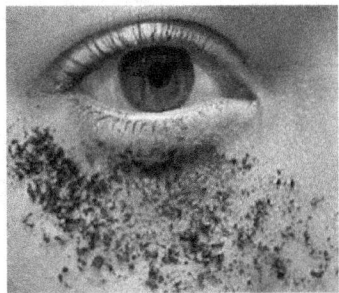
This £3 Method Removes Your Eye-Bags & Wrinkles in 2 Minutes

This Video Will Soon Be Banned. Watch Before It's Deleted

5 Tricks to Learn Spanish (or Any Other Language)

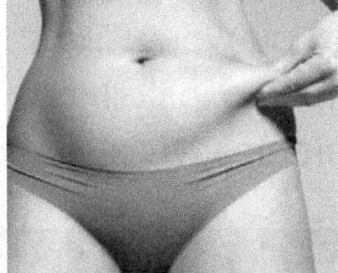
No Need to Diet or Go to the Gym If You Do This Before Bed

They often link to a blog post or article just like the one they are serving on.

So, they can appear to be a little less "salesy" and a bit more user friendly for people looking to just kill some time for example.

How much can I expect to make from Native Ads?

In general, these do not pay as high per click as Adsense ads do. I have run these on a website of mine for several years and I can say that the results I have show around a 1.2% click through rate.

What does this mean?

Broadly speaking, this means that for every 1000 visitors 12 people will click on the ads.

May not sound like a lot but it soon ads up.

There are many native ad networks that will happily accept your blog or website to publish their ads on and once you are familiar with Wordpress for example the installation of them is very simple.

If you would like to read further on native ads and how to install them on your blog, I wrote a detailed article with a video walking you through it.

Native ads training: sideincomeman.com/native

The ad network I recommend you use is content.ad. The reason I like this network is because they also pay out for any affiliate sales that go through the ads. Some of the ads will have an offer on the page people are clicking through to.

If that visitor then goes on to buy that product you get a cut of the sale price as a commission.

As you can see here just 13 clicks generated over $53.

Native ad networks can be a great way to build up some extra passive income. In fact, many people use these alongside their Adsense ads to generate two streams. Obviously, a user can only click on one ad at a time so it's difficult to say whether one ad network or two perform better.

Just test them out on your site and see what works for you.

It should also be noted that if you intend to make a site which gets a nice growing audience you could in fact sell it for a very handsome sum!

#8 Voice Over Translation

User Level

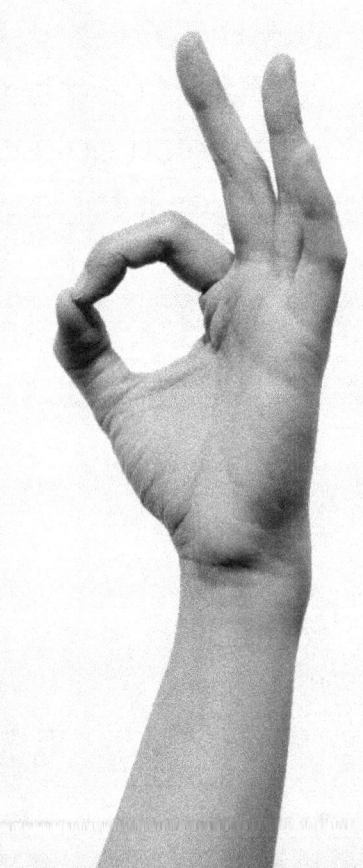

"Language translation is a very popular market with many hungry buyers waiting to buy from you!"

Fiverr as you may or may not know is a website where you can offer up your services and find clients from their hungry buying traffic.

It originally started out as a site where you could only charge $5 for your service. Hence the name. However, it has evolved massively now, and people are making some serious money on there.

No longer do you only have to offer up your service for $5. You can scale it up and offer hundreds of dollars for each "gig" you set up if you so wish.

Anyway, on to this specifically.

Language translation is a very popular market and there are many hungry buyers needing this service.

If you know a second language you could offer up your services on there by translating peoples written blog articles for example.

Another area is doing voice overs in a different language. People here are making really good money and it does not have to be a long translation too.

Just 75 – 100 words can get you around $50. How long would it take you to translate that amount of words into another language if you are fluent in it anyway?

Not too long I would imagine.

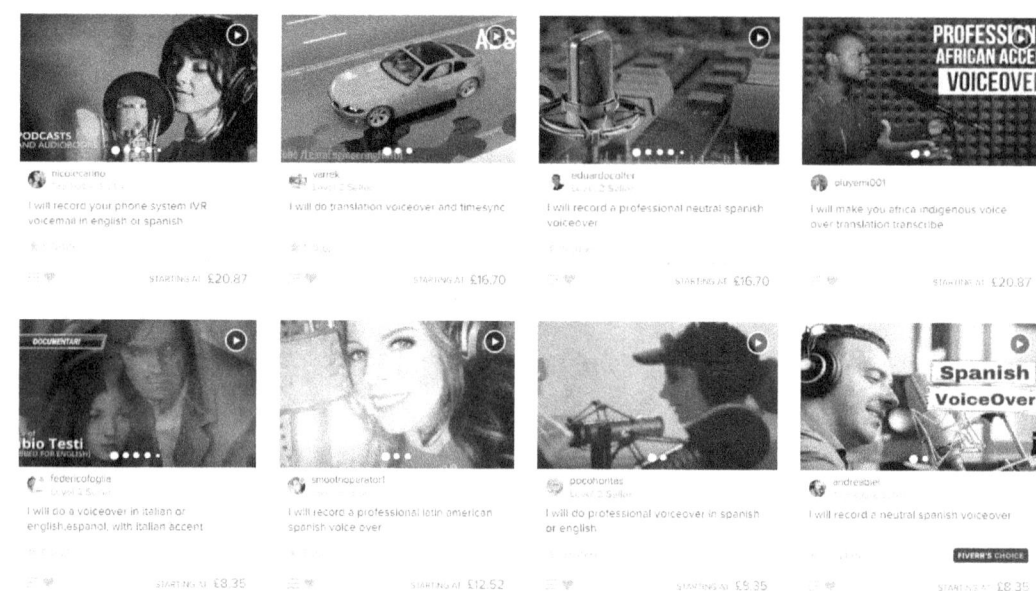

Sure, there has to be a touch of professionalism to it and talking into a microphone is not going to be for everybody, but I am sure there are many people who read this that could do this.

If talking is not your thing then how about written translation? This will obviously take you a little longer, but I am sure once you have a system in place you can maximise this side hustle.

I would say though that gig-wise you would probably earn more for your time doing the voice overs than the article translation, but you could argue that the written one is an easier side hustle to get going with.

#9 Write For Cash

User Level

"There are tons of websites across all niches willing to pay you for your written work"

If writing is your thing then there are a whole host of sites that are willing to pay for your services. However, when just starting out writing gigs can be a tough journey, but if you stick with it and get some regular clients the rewards can be very good indeed.

That last part is the key, regular clients.

You want to try and land a few sites that will pay you for your work on a recurring basis. If you can land a job writing 2 x blog posts each month for a blog for $200 then that is a good start.

But it's finding them first. All of these clients use many of the sites I will list below so you have to offer up your services there. Then it's all about getting found out.

You should promote yourself on social media, offer your services out on LinkedIn, Facebook, Twitter basically anywhere where you have an account.

Post up your work in forums and in relevant Facebook groups.

I find with writing gigs you have to do the hard work in the beginning. Sometimes you may even have to work for low returns in order to get some clients.

If you done a few Fiverr gigs at the minimum price just to get started this would land you a few gigs and then you could blow the client away with your quality and switch to a permanent monthly side hustle should they require it.

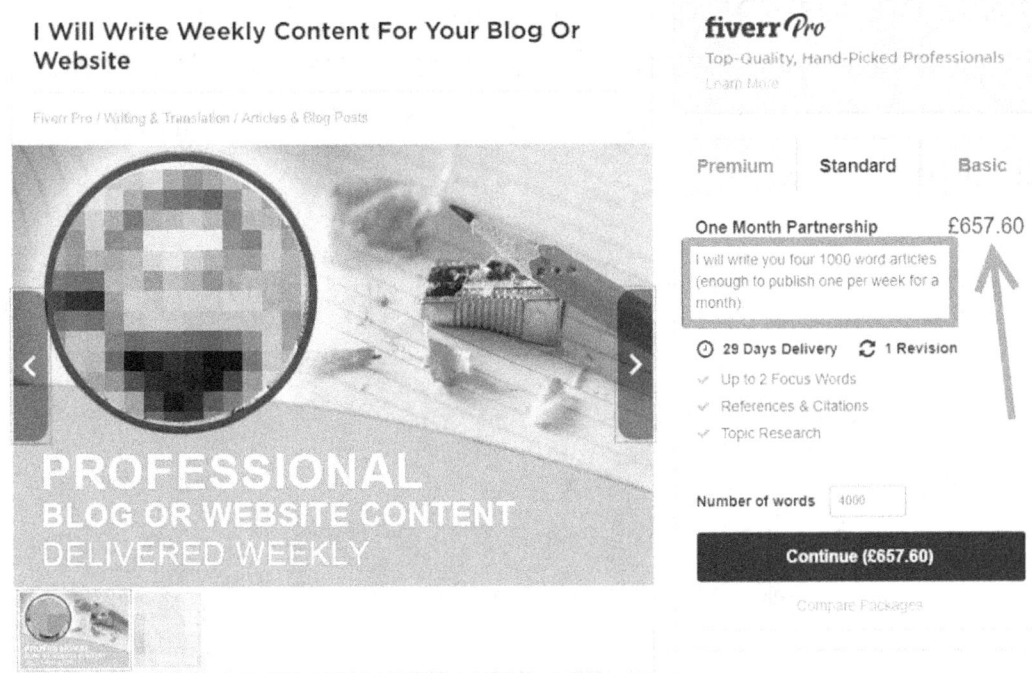

Where can I offer up my writing services and get paid?

As I mentioned above Fiverr is not the only place to earn money writing articles. Below is a list of places you can also earn by writing.

A little word of warning though – not all of these sites will be for everyone.

- **Fiverr** -Low entry gigs from $5 for short articles, once you build up your rep you can pitch higher.

- **Upwork** - Good site for landing long term paying clients, but often a race to the bottom for bidding.

- **TextBroker** - Good site that pays per word, the higher the quality the higher the pay.

These are just the tip of the iceberg here really. The list goes on, you need a bit of hustle for this. You have to pitch your articles to sites to see if they want to publish your work.

Use this search to find more sites and gold!

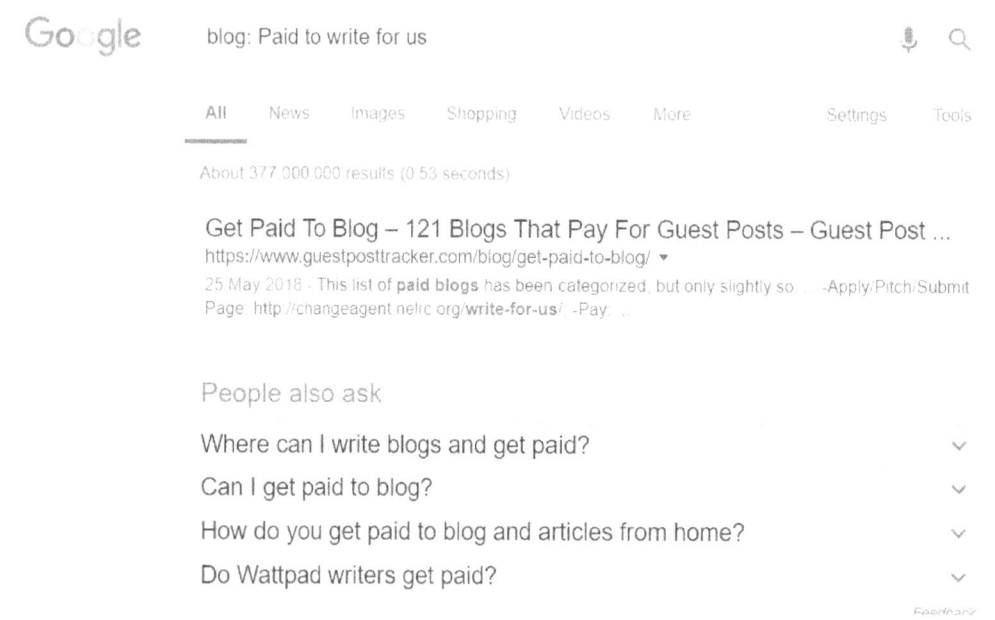

Remember there are two ways to do this. Offer up your gigs on sites and wait for customers to come to you or head over to the many websites on offer and pitch your work to them. There are also job boards on some websites which allow you to quote for your job before you get it.

For more pages that will pay you to write for them head over to the blog!

Here are a few more niche specific ones. Always check what content they are after before submitting.

- **Chicken Soup For The Soul** – Heart-warming stories, true stories, even poetry. They pay up to $200 per accepted submission.

- **Readers Digest** – Short stories submission, any true story about you. If accepted for publication they pay you $100

- **Woodworking Magazine** – This site is self-explanatory. It wants articles on woodworking as a hobby or career. They encourage new people to the craft to submit too, even if you are not a pro! Pay up to $250 per 600-word article if accepted.

#10 Sing Songs Badly!

User Level

"This is a bit of fun really, but you will be amazed at what people do to make some extra cash!"

How would you like to make money by singing Happy Birthday? This is no joke. What would you say if I said there are people making serious money just by singing Happy Birthday to people by making a silly video for them?

You may or may not fancy this as a side hustle for yourself but what I want this post to do is hopefully give you an idea of more obscure methods to earn money online.

With the ever-growing places now to host your own services 'gigs' like this are becoming more and more popular.

For these gigs I have been surfing through the more alternative sections on Fiverr.

If you have been living under a rock for the last few years and don't know what Fiverr is it's a website allowing you to provide services for people on just about anything. Or, you can buy too.

I do both, well not so much of the selling these days but I used to.

It's both a great way to make money and a great source for getting jobs done for you.

Whether you want some writing doing, maybe some custom graphics made or maybe you want a new voiceover for a video. Then this is the place.

But – not only does it offer professional services it also offers some more bizarre and slightly left field gigs. You can get things like Tarot card readings, impressions, prank videos, your message on.... plus loads more. Some VERY bizarre and adult ones too!

Health, Nutrition & Fitness

Astrology & Readings

Spiritual & Healing

Family & Genealogy

Collectibles

Greeting Cards & Videos

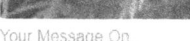
Your Message On

Viral Videos

Pranks & Stunts

If you have not got an account with Fiverr then I HIGHLY recommend you get one. It will come in very handy and there are some great sellers offering fantastic services for just $5 (That's why it's called Fiverr).

So, How Do You Make Money Singing Happy Birthday?

I have outlined 5 gigs here from people on the site making money from singing. They are all doing really well in their chosen categories.

They are offering a singing/personal message service to some degree. It is hard to tell their exact earnings but based on their reviews I will take a guess on each one of their totals for just that gig.

In some cases, the earnings that I have predicted could actually be LOWER than what they are really getting because not everyone will leave a review. Most sellers have several gigs up and with a minimum price tag of $5 on each one you can see how they can quickly mount up into a very nice side income.

The Dancing Fruitman (Estimated Earnings $2000 – $3000)

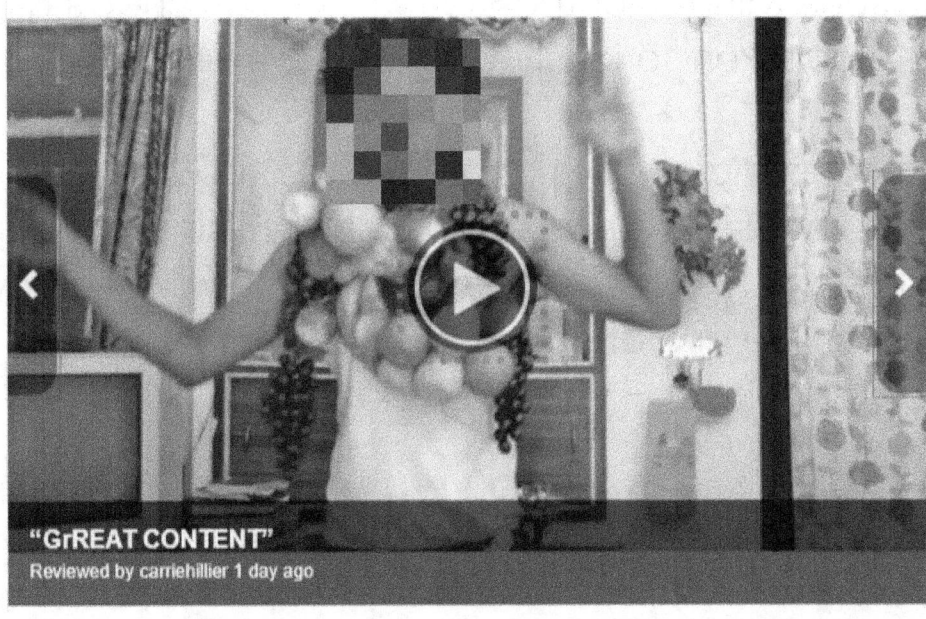

This guy is hilarious. He wears a fruit costume and will say anything you want when he is wearing it.
But, a common request seems to be the Happy Birthday song. This one gig of his has over 240 reviews at the time of writing this.

It is not his only gig too; he also provides alternative versions in different costumes such as the vegetable suit!

His global reviews up to this point are over 900! This means he has made well over $7000 so not bad for a guy singing in suits based on foods.

I say excellent hustle. It might not be to everyone's taste but it's a bit of fun and this guy is doing great from it. Top work!

The Birthday Shower Man (Estimated Earnings $1500 – $2000)

Certainly not everyone's cup of tea but with earnings almost certainly over the $1500 mark this chap's gig has to be taken seriously (sort of).

For a basic gig starting at around $15 he will do a simple shout out, for around $20 he will sing any song you like and for the top premium gig he will sing any song you like and drink a shot of gunpowder moonshine liquor – whatever that is!

This guy's total review count for all his gigs are over 500 reviews, multiply this by his lowest price gig at $15 and that gives a nice revenue so far of around $6500.

Not bad for singing a few songs in the shower.

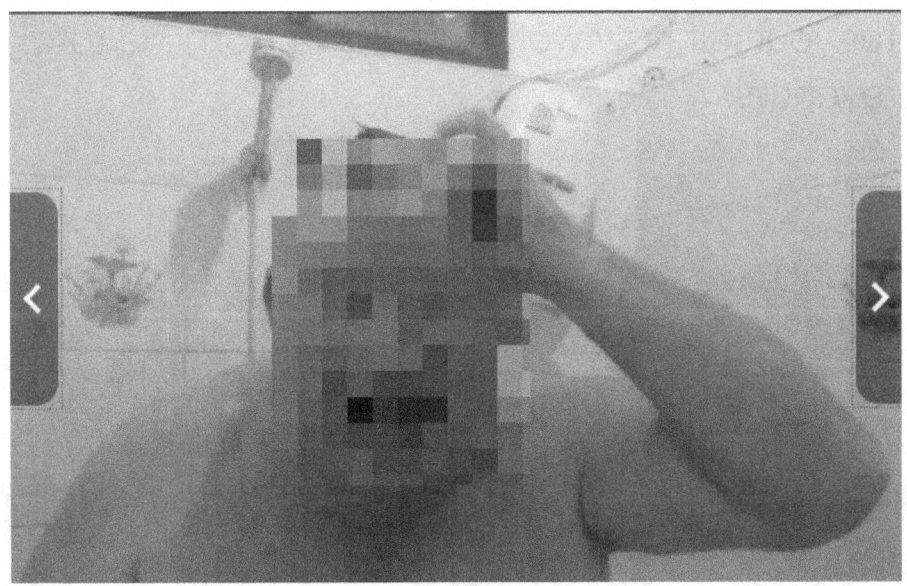

Not sure about the gunpowder shots but keep up with the singing!

Jesus Will Say Anything (Estimated Earnings $15000+)

The son of God is on Fiverr and he wants to make the perfect gig for you. He will say or sing anything with a whole host of backgrounds and special effects starting from $10 and working all the way up to the hundreds of dollars per gig.

This guy has been a Fiverr sensation and claims to have had over 7000 orders for his Jesus gigs.

Even if he was only selling them at $10 you can work out for yourself how well he is doing from his total gig revenue.

Although strictly speaking this is not an exclusive Happy Birthday gig, he will do it so it makes it onto the list. And because his earnings are pretty amazing from it how could I not include it!

Old Man Steve And The Birthday Banana (Estimated Earnings $1000)

I don't know about you, but I find it quite impressive earning over $1000 talking into a banana. This guy is brilliant, he will sing happy birthday whilst pretending to use a banana as a telephone.

Crazy, yet funny. And it would appear I am not the only one who thinks so. He has had over 100 reviews on just this gig, and he starts his pricing around $10 so not too bad at all!

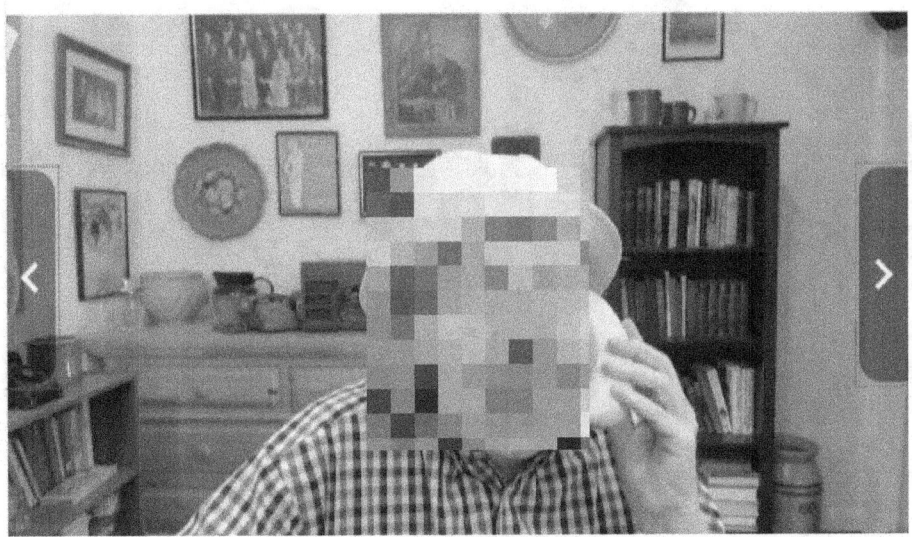

So, for those of you who think the only way to earn some extra cash is to sell stuff on eBay think again!

The Vietnam Birthday Singer (Estimated Earnings $1000+)

Arguably my pick of the bunch. Very unique it has to be said. Specialising only in singing Happy Birthday this guy all the way from Vietnam has racked up a healthy 130 reviews at the time of writing this post for his birthday song gig.

Nothing else here, just a simple birthday song gig. With his own style of course.

Excellent work to this chap and all the Fiverr birthday singers.

My Thoughts On This

Now for something a bit more serious. Now I know some people reading this will be saying "That's ridiculous, you are not going to get me in front of a camera doing that!" – and that's fine.

What this hustle is meant to do is open your eyes up to the endless possibilities out there to earn some extra money.

You just have to think a little outside the box.

I have massive respect for these guys, they have taken an opportunity (the internet) and created something that people will happily exchange money for.

It's brilliant.

I used to run Fiverr gigs (not signing happy birthday songs) but more of a marketing gig. And it got loads of sales and done really well for a while.

Fiverr is a GREAT platform if you have a skill that people will pay you for.

Gone are the days of just offering $5 for a gig, people are earning serious money now on this platform.

Fiverr is a GREAT platform if you have a skill that people will pay you for. You can offer everything from:

- Making Facebook Headers
- Making Logos
- Writing Gigs
- Voiceovers
- Proof Reading
- Pinterest Marketing
- YouTube Headers
- Twitter Headers
- Small Crafts
- Business Card Designs
- Flyers
- Video Intros

The list goes on and on, I have mainly focused on digital tasks here but as you can see from this post Fiverr is not just a place for people with digital expertise.

Maybe you could become the next Banana singing sensation!?

Or maybe not.....

That market is covered.

...Over To You

Now it's your turn, there is enough in this book to get you started on your side hustle journey. Whether it is reselling on eBay or starting a blog there is something in here which you can get started with today.

Of course there are hundreds of side hustles you can do these days, both offline and online and loads will be covered on the blog but this book is aimed at the starter and hopefully one day you can feature on the Spotlights on the blog and I will be interviewing you and you can share your story of how your side hustle ended up replacing your full time income!

Join The Movement.

Keep on hustling....

John | SideIncomeMan.com

Notes

Your side hustle ideas and thoughts!

"If you run into a wall, don't turn around and give up. Figure out how to climb it"

SideIncomeMan.com

www.ingramcontent.com/pod-product-compliance
Lightning Source LLC
Chambersburg PA
CBHW080512220526
45465CB00006B/2455